People today yearn for deepened connections with family and friends. *Heavenly Friends* broadens that longing in a unique way: we meet a variety of saints and other holy people who surround us, our heavenly friends and family in the Communion of Saints.

We encounter these friends in heaven through reflections on treasured art; their lives—their ordinariness and holiness—come alive to us through the beauty and inspiration of icons. These icons and the accompanying reflections and prayers connect with our real-life experiences today, such as times of worry or fear, our desire to be generous and caring, the times we're called to forgive, the challenge to stand up for what we believe.

The value of being connected with friends; an interest in family trees; the power of images (sometimes more than words): these are intriguing to children and young people as well. *Heavenly Friends* responds to these curiosities in a unique way.

Heavenly Friends will help us all—adults and children—make new friends who are always there to inspire, to guide, and to encourage.

JANET SCHAEFFLER, OP, *author of A Treasury of Marian Prayers: A Handbook of Popular Devotions*

Heavenly Friends is a simple and beautiful way to engage in the art of visually reflecting on the sacred, otherwise known as *visio divina*. The saints featured were obviously selected with care and representative of the diversity of God's people and the times in which they lived. With short bios and artistic commentary, *Heavenly Friends* is a wonderful resource for inspiring wonder.

DR. MATTHEW HALBACH, *author of The Wounded Body of Christ: A Parish Group Discussion Guide on Abuse in the Catholic Church*

heavenly friends

An Introduction to the Beauty of Icons

FR. WILLIAM
HART MCNICHOLS
and KATHY HENDRICKS

TWENTY-THIRD PUBLICATIONS
twentythirdpublications.com

ACKNOWLEDGMENTS

Special thanks to Marjory McNichols Wilson for her invaluable assistance with the transfer of the icons.

All Images ©William Hart McNichols
www.FrBillMcNichols-SacredImages.com

TWENTY-THIRD PUBLICATIONS, A division of Bayard, Inc.
One Montauk Avenue, Suite 200 • New London, CT 06320
(860) 437-3012 or (800) 321-0411 • www.twentythirdpublications.com

Copyright © 2019 William Hart McNichols and Kathy Hendricks.
All rights reserved. No part of this publication may be reproduced in any manner without prior written permission of the publisher. Write to the Permissions Editor.

ISBN: 978-1-62785-423-8
Printed in the U.S.A.

 A division of Bayard, Inc.

TABLE *of* CONTENTS

2

Thérèse of Lisieux

4

Louis IX, King of France

6

Rose of Lima

8

Tarcisius

10

Dorothy Stang

12
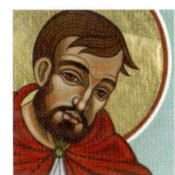
Joseph

14

Dorothy Day

16

Francis of Assisi

18

Isidro & Maria

20

Francisco Marto

22

Maria Goretti

24

Hildegard of Bingen & Ignatius Loyola

"I give praise to you, Father, for although you have hidden these things from the wise and learned, you have revealed them to the childlike."

Matthew 11:25

INTRODUCTION

Icons bring us into the presence of holy people by inviting conversation with them in the midst of ordinary life. Along with other forms of sacred art, they stir the imagination by presenting visual images of holy people in ways that resonate with our own lives. Icons offer particular opportunities for deepening an appreciation of these heavenly friends through something visually beautiful and symbolically meaningful. While icons might first appear sad or serious, further reflection draws us deeper into their beauty and depth.

Heavenly Friends is an introduction to stories about saints and other holy people through the use of icons by Father William (Bill) Hart McNichols. Each section contains an icon of a holy person and an accompanying story, written by Kathy Hendricks, about the person's life and spirituality. The figures have been chosen to connect in a particular way with a life experience. Father Bill offers insights into the symbols that he incorporated into the icon so as to expand appreciation of its artistry and meaning. A brief practice of *visio divina*—"sacred seeing"—leads the viewer into prayer and reflection. Ideas for celebrating the holy person's feast—the day on which his or her life is celebrated—are also included.

The stories are told in simple fashion so that each one might also be shared with children. In addition to reading the book with children, parents and catechists might leave it in a special place dedicated to prayer in the home or classroom so that the child has access to continued reflection with the icons. In such a way everyone's friendship with these heavenly figures grows, as does their intimacy with God, whose light and love are ever-present. We are all called to be saints. In reading about and turning to these holy people in prayer, we learn how to listen to our own particular calling toward sanctity and God's grace.

Thérèse of the Child Jesus and the Holy Face

OCTOBER 1

As a young child, Thérèse Martin developed a deep love for Jesus that grew throughout her life. Her mother, Zelie, died when she was only four, so Thérèse was cared for by her four older sisters and her father, Louis. When she was only fifteen, Thérèse knew she wanted to follow her sisters by entering a Carmelite convent where she could dedicate her life to prayer. She was so young that she needed special permission from Pope Leo to become a religious sister. Life in the convent was not always easy.

Thérèse followed what she called the "little way," by doing small things each day to increase her love for God and for those around her. She died when she was only twenty-four years old and left behind a journal that described this way of prayer and holiness.

Fr. Bill's Icon

Thérèse promised that, when she died, she would send down a shower of roses from heaven. In one hand you see her shredding a white rose and dropping the petals to us, a sign of her answer to our prayers. In her other hand, she holds a picture of the Holy Face of Jesus, an image that drew her into prayer. The Child Jesus, to whom Thérèse was devoted, clings to her as if needing her help.

Thérèse is a saint to whom we can turn for her prayers when we, too, are in need of help.

Praying with the Icon

Look for a moment at the icon. What do you see? What help do you need? Ask Thérèse to pray for those needs. On her feast day make a special effort to practice the "little way" through acts of generosity and caring.

Saint Thérèse, help me to turn to Jesus in my prayers the way you did. May I follow your little way by showing my love for God and for others in what I say and do each day.

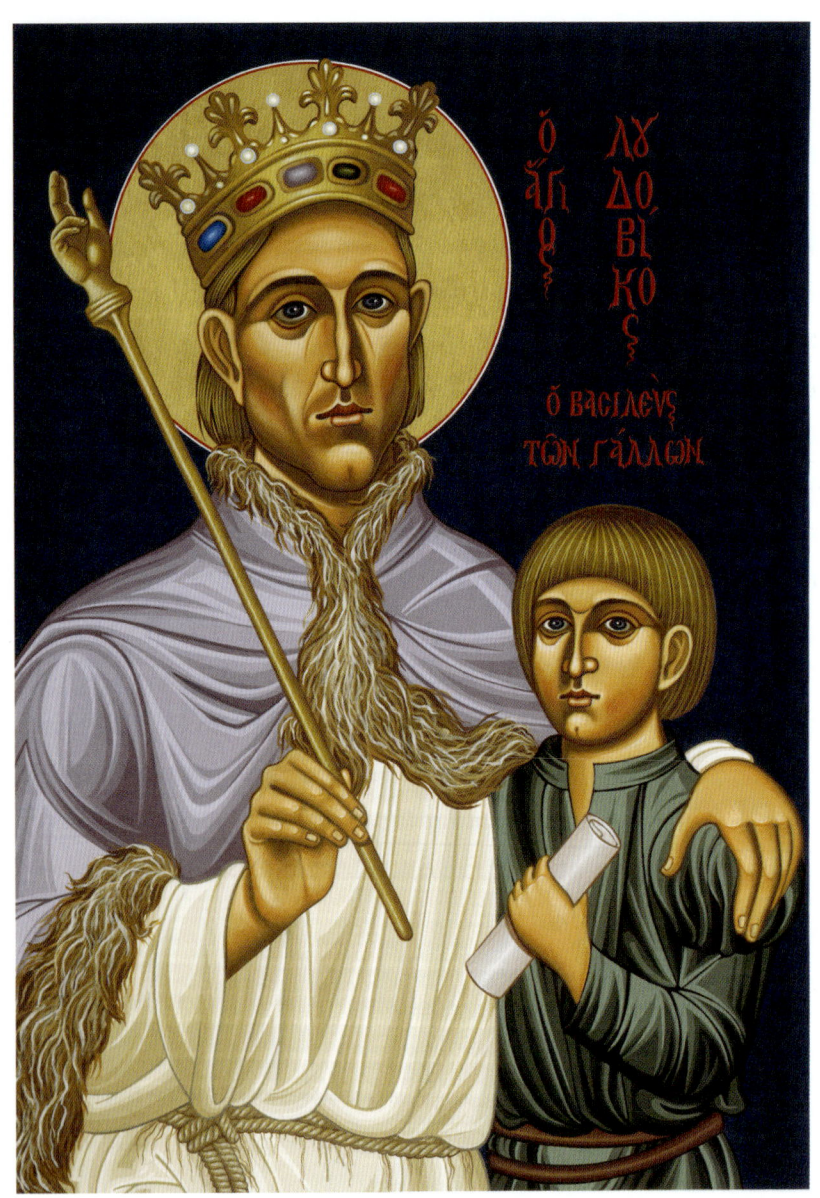

Louis IX, King of France

AUGUST 25

When he was crowned the king of France, Louis IX promised to reign in the way God would want. He kept this promise by bringing peace and justice to the country. He reformed the way in which people were brought to trial for crimes, making the system more just. Louis showed special care for those who were poor. He founded hospitals and visited those who were sick. He built beautiful churches as well as libraries and orphanages for the people of France. He and his wife, Queen Margaret, had eleven children, whom they loved very much. As a king, Louis was not perfect but he was fair and respectful of his people. As a father and husband, he was loving and faithful.

Fr. Bill's Icon

Louis is dressed in a soft purple robe, the color of Advent and Lent. During these sacred seasons anyone who came to him for food was fed, sometimes served by the king himself. He wears a simple rope around his waist, just like his patron saint, Francis of Assisi, who cared for the poor. His son, Philip, holds a letter from his father. In it, Louis encouraged his son to love God with all his heart and strength.

Praying with the Icon

Look at how Louis has his arm draped around Philip's shoulder. It shows the love and protection he wanted to give his son. Imagine God holding you in his loving and protective embrace. Ask Louis to help you show love and compassion. On his feast day, write a letter to God expressing your love and faith.

Saint Louis, you were a fair and just king who gave generously to those who were sick and hungry. Pray for all fathers and their sons so that they grow in love and respect for one another.

Rose of Lima

AUGUST 23

Rose was born in Lima, Peru, and given the name Isabel Flores de Oliva. She was so beautiful that she was nicknamed "Rose," a name she took at her confirmation. When she was quite young she knew that she wanted to enter a religious order but her parents objected. They wanted her to marry and raise a family. Her mother was especially worried about the extreme penance that Rose practiced, afraid that she was doing great harm to herself. Rose persisted in her desire to practice her faith and became a Third Order Dominican. It was said that roses bloomed in her garden all year round. She sold the roses to help her family. Her father let her use one of the rooms in their house to care for homeless children, the elderly, and the sick. When she died, all of the important people in Lima came to honor her at her funeral.

Fr. Bill's Icon

See how Rose is standing on the tip of North and South America, for which she is the patroness. Even though she lived a humble and simple life and was often ridiculed for her faith, she stands tall and looks with love on the world below her. Roses, symbols of her inner and outer beauty, fall from her hands onto the world below her.

Praying with the Icon

Look at the gentle love on Rose's face as she gazes upon the world. Even though Rose suffered ridicule from her family and friends for her call to follow God, she remained loving, kind, and generous. Ask Rose to pray for you when you find it hard to be generous or caring. On her feast day go out of your way to show kindness to someone who may face ridicule by others.

Saint Rose, you listened to the call of God in your life.
Pray for all mothers and daughters as they live out their faith
and show concern for one another.

Tarcisius
AUGUST 15

Christians who lived soon after the time of Jesus' death and resurrection faced great persecution for their faith. In order to meet and pray together, Christians in Rome met in secret. Afterward, a deacon carried Holy Communion to those in prison. One day, when there was no deacon to send, Tarcisius, a boy of twelve, went instead. On his way he was stopped by other boys who wanted him to join them in playing a game. When they saw that he was carrying something, they became more insistent. Tarcisius refused to let go of his sacred task, and the boys started to beat him until an older Christian drove them away. Tarcisius was carried back home but his wounds were too great and he died along the way. Although not much more is known about this young martyr he is revered today for his faith and his courage in carrying out such a dangerous task.

Fr. Bill's Icon

You can see how Tarcisius has his hands crossed over a small pouch in which he carries Holy Communion for the imprisoned Christians. Imagine how frightened he was to be surrounded by bullies who made fun of his devotion to his faith and then beat him viciously. Even so his crossed hands show his willingness to die so that others might be nourished in their faith through the Eucharist.

Praying with the Icon

Look at the look of peace in the eyes of Tarcisius. He was bullied in the worst way possible but remained steadfast in his love for Jesus. When you feel afraid to stand up for what you believe, ask Tarcisius to pray for you and to inspire you with his courage. On his feast day carry the love of Christ to someone who needs a friend.

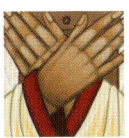

Saint Tarcisius, you were very young, and yet you remained faithful to your love for Jesus. Pray for those who are bullied for what they believe is right and good.

Dorothy Stang

FEBRUARY 12

Dorothy Stang grew up on a farm in Ohio with her eight brothers and sisters. At the age of seventeen she entered the religious community of the Sisters of Notre Dame de Namur. After teaching school for a few years, she began her lifelong work with poor farmers in Brazil. She was especially concerned about the way in which the Amazon rainforest was being destroyed by those wanting to use the land for their own profit. Not only did this destroy a precious part of God's creation, but the stripping of the forest took away the small plots of land worked by poor farmers and peasants. Sister Dorothy's work put her in great danger. One morning, as she walked to a meeting about the rights of these poor workers, she was met by two gunmen. She took out her Bible, her only weapon, and began reading the Beatitudes. She gave her life following the call of Christ to care for the poor and to stand for justice.

Fr. Bill's Icon

Sister Dorothy understood the importance of keeping the rainforest from being destroyed. Beside her are the Portuguese words, "The death of the forest is the death of our lives." Trees of the Amazon rainforest appear behind her. Even though her life was threatened by those who wanted to cut down the trees for their own profit, Sister Dorothy stood strong in her faith and in her commitment to the poor people whose land was being taken away.

Praying with the Icon

Look at the determination in Sister Dorothy's face and her raised arm. She knew that speaking out endangered her life and yet she continued her work in protecting the rainforest and the rights of the poor. Ask Dorothy to remind you to give thanks for the gifts of God's creation. On her feast day you might visit a garden, park, or other place of natural beauty.

Holy Dorothy, you gave your life for your belief in God and for the poor people of the Brazilian rainforest. Pray for all of those who care for God's creation and for those needing someone strong to stand up for them.

Joseph
MARCH 19

Joseph was married to Mary and given the responsibility of caring for her and her son, Jesus. One night an angel came to Joseph in a dream and told him to take Mary and Jesus to Egypt where they would be safe from King Herod, who ordered the killing of all boys under the age of two in Jewish families in Bethlehem. They stayed in Egypt until an angel told Joseph it was safe to return home. The family settled in the town of Nazareth where Joseph worked as a carpenter and taught Jesus these same skills. We don't know much more about Joseph's life, but we honor him for his protective love of Mary and Jesus and his great faith in God. Even though he did not always understand what God asked of him, he was willing to obey and to put the needs of his family first.

Fr. Bill's Icon

Joseph's cloak partly covers the halo of the child Jesus. It's a way of showing that Jesus was not yet ready to show who he was to the world. Both figures carry a staff and Joseph appears to be guiding Jesus forward. He appears strong but also warm and caring. No wonder so many people turn to Joseph for his prayers for their families.

Praying with the Icon

Look at the way Joseph's arm wraps around Jesus' shoulder in a gesture of supportive love. When you are afraid or uncertain, ask Joseph to pray for protection from harm and for guidance on the path of your life. On his feast day thank someone who protects and cares for you.

Saint Joseph, you listened to God's call to protect and care for Jesus and Mary. Pray for all families who are victims of violence, war, and terror.

Dorothy Day

NOVEMBER 29

Dorothy Day was born in New York City in 1897 and began working for peace and justice as a young woman. She started out as a writer and later founded special homes for those in need. When her daughter, Tamar Teresa, was born, Dorothy brought her to a Catholic church to be baptized. This ignited her belief in God, which grew deeper as she continued her work with the poor. Her friend Peter Maurin shared her faith and her commitment to peace and justice. Together, they started a newspaper called *The Catholic Worker* in which they wrote about serving the poor in the way of Jesus. Dorothy understood that it is important to feed a person's soul as well as the body. She wanted those who came for food and shelter to be treated with love, respect, and hospitality. Catholic Worker houses continue today to serve the homeless across the United States and in countries around the world.

Fr. Bill's Icon

Dorothy is dressed in a simple brown robe, the color worn by Saint Francis of Assisi, because of how she followed his example of love and care for the poor. Snow falls on the city behind her. Imagine living on the streets when it is cold and snowy. Dorothy insisted that all of those who entered the Catholic Worker houses be greeted with warmth, welcome, and respect for their human dignity.

Praying with the Icon

Look at the determination in Dorothy's face. She was a strong woman who could be stubborn and demanding as well as kind and compassionate. Ask her to pray for you when you find it hard to be courageous and to serve others. On her feast day let her inspire you to be welcoming and kind toward others.

Holy Dorothy, you understood that all people should be treated with respect and compassion. Pray for those who have no homes and the people who reach out to care for them.

Francis of Assisi

OCTOBER 4

Francis was the son of a wealthy merchant from the town of Assisi in Italy. He lived a carefree life until he became a soldier and was held prisoner during a war with a neighboring country. After finally returning home, Francis began to have dreams and visions. One day he was praying and heard the voice of Christ telling him to rebuild the church. At first, he thought this meant repairing the rundown church of San Damiano. Later he understood that his call was to follow the way of Jesus in the gospels. This meant caring for the poor, treating all of creation as sacred, and loving both friend and enemy. He inspired others who joined him in living simply, preaching the gospel, and making prayer a vital part of their lives.

Fr. Bill's Icon

Sometimes, when someone like Francis loves Jesus so much, they even want to experience his suffering. You can see that his hands and feet are bleeding from wounds like the ones Jesus suffered when he was nailed to the cross. An angel-like figure called a seraph rises just above his praying hands. This shows how Francis felt both the pain of Christ as well as his great love.

Praying with the Icon

Look at the simple clothes Francis is wearing. Although he was born into a wealthy family, he chose to live simply and to serve those who were poor, sick, and unwanted. Whenever you do something kind and loving you are building the church in the way that Francis did. Ask for his prayers to make your heart loving and generous. On his feast day spend time with a pet, or play or walk outside and enjoy the glories of God's creation.

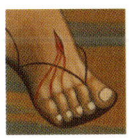

Saint Francis, you saw God's goodness in all of creation. Pray for the protection of animals and for the well-being of all people on earth.

Isidro & Maria

MAY 15 [*Isidro*]

SEPTEMBER 9 [*Maria*]

Isidro and Maria were a married couple and parents of a little boy. They lived in Spain, where Isidro worked on the farm of a wealthy man. Although they were very poor, the couple shared what food they had with others who were in need. Isidro also loved animals and made sure they were treated well on the farm. After their little boy died, Isidro and Maria turned to God for comfort and continued to show compassion and generosity toward those who were poor. Although they lived simple lives as farmers, Isidro and Maria found joy in being a family and in sharing what they had with others.

Fr. Bill's Icon

Maria and Isidro stand together with their little boy, forming a lovely picture of a family. Their son holds a shovel and the couple are dressed in the simple clothes of Spanish peasants. They hold each other in a circle of love. No matter how much or how little we own, our most precious gift is the love we share with others.

Praying with the Icon

Look at the family gathered together. It was very sad for Isidro and Maria when their son died, and yet they continued to love God and share generously with others. They show us the joy that comes from being a family. When you are sad over the loss of someone you love, ask them to pray for your heart to heal. On their feast days show your love for your family by surprising them with an act of kindness or generosity.

Saints Isidro and Maria, you were poor and yet you shared what you had with others. Pray for families who have no homes or very little to eat or who struggle to keep themselves well.

Francisco Marto

FEBRUARY 20

Francisco Marto grew up with his sister, Jacinta, and his cousin, Lucia, near the town of Fatima in Portugal. Francisco had a tender heart and a love of music. He cared so much for animals that he once paid a boy to release a bird from captivity. One day the three children began seeing visions of an angel and then of Mary, the Mother of Jesus, in a field where their families tended sheep. Mary told them to return to the spot each month, where she appeared again and urged them to pray that all people would turn their hearts toward God. At first the authorities didn't believe the children and treated them harshly. As news of the visions spread, people came to pray on the same spot. Francisco and Jacinta were taken ill by a terrible flu that spread through the country. They died with a peaceful trust in God's great love for them.

Fr. Bill's Icon

The spinning sun behind Francisco is what pilgrims saw when they visited the site where the visions took place. Francisco's hands are folded in prayer and his face looks troubled. He once said that he wanted to comfort God who must be sad over the way people turn away from his love.

Praying with the Icon

Look at the sadness and worry in Francisco's face. He remembered how Mary told the children to pray for peace in the world and for an end to all wars. Ask Francisco for his prayers when you feel anxious and afraid. On his feast day see how you can bring peace to others through kind and caring words and actions.

Saint Francisco, you wanted all people to turn their hearts to God. Pray for peace in our world and especially for children who live in war-torn countries.

Maria Goretti

JULY 6

Maria Goretti was the daughter of a poor Italian farm worker and his wife. Her father died when Maria was only nine years old, so she had to manage the household while her mother and brothers worked in the fields. One day she was sitting outside of her house when a young man named Alessandro attacked her. Even though she fought and pleaded with him to stop, he stabbed her fourteen times. Before she died in the hospital, she told her mother that she forgave her attacker. Alessandro was sent to prison for his crime. While there he had a dream that Maria appeared to him and gave him fourteen flowers—one for each of her stab wounds. This changed his life completely. When he was released, he went to Maria's mother to ask for her forgiveness and spent the rest of his life trying to do good.

Fr. Bill's Icon

Maria is a young girl with her hands pressed close to her heart. Even though she was viciously attacked, she forgave Alessandro before she died. To forgive doesn't mean we excuse the terrible things another person has done; and children who face harm or abuse need to know they can tell a trusted adult. Maria's story teaches us how forgiveness can change another person and inspire others to be merciful.

Praying with the Icon

Look at how Maria's hands are crossed over her heart. It is as if she is both protecting herself and praying for mercy. Ask Maria for her prayers when you need protection from harm. On her feast day look for a chance to ask for forgiveness and to show mercy to others.

Saint Maria Goretti, you were attacked in a terrible way. Pray for all children to be protected from abuse and harm.

Hildegard of Bingen & Ignatius Loyola

SEPTEMBER 17 [*Hildegard*]

JULY 31 [*Ignatius*]

It was evident from the time she was a little girl that Hildegard was special. She saw clearly how all of God's creation worked together in harmony. As she grew older she began to compose beautiful music, write books, and use various plants and herbs to heal people's illnesses. Ignatius also had a gift for seeing God's work in the world. After being wounded as a soldier during a war, he read books about the saints and had a vision of Mary, the Mother of God. He then began to guide others in seeing how God was alive and present in their lives. Even though they lived at different times, these two great saints inspired others to discover the joy of God's love.

Fr. Bill's Icon

Ignatius comes forward to give Hildegard a cross of wood. As she blesses it, with the child Jesus at her side, it turns green with life. The harp sits at her feet. Rays of light shine down upon her. Both Hildegard and Ignatius saw the light of God's love fill their lives and sought to help others find that light.

Praying with the Icon

Look at Hildegard's hand resting on the shoulder of the child Jesus and how Ignatius reaches his hand down to him. It is as if they are encouraging him in some way. Hildegard and Ignatius continue to inspire people. Ask them to help you discover your gifts and how you might share them with others. On Hildegard's feast, join in her love of God's creation by listening to music or visiting a natural place of beauty. On the feast of Ignatius, read a story about someone who will inspire you to share God's light with others.

Saints Hildegard and Ignatius, you both used your gifts to help others discover God's light and love in their lives. Pray that all people come to recognize the gifts they have to inspire others in their faith.

 HERALDED BY *TIME* MAGAZINE AS "AMONG THE MOST FAMOUS CREATORS OF CHRISTIAN ICONIC IMAGERY IN THE WORLD," Father William Hart McNichols creates paintings inspired by a centuries-old tradition, masterfully brought to the present through a thoughtful selection of subjects. Father McNichols not only honors a holy person or event, but he also represents symbolic individuals from various religious and lay backgrounds, figures from popular culture, and people well-known for making an impact in social justice causes. Neither the icons nor the saints represented in his works are meant to be worshiped, but rather are to be seen as "windows" into the heavenly realm. The beauty of these images will call you to learn more about each icon's inspiring story.

frbillmcnichols-sacredimages.com